WARRIOR HEART

A journey to healing and freedom

By: Katrina Crain

ISBN: 9798646934667

DEDICATION

I want to dedicate this book to my daughter, Kira. My whole life, I dreamed of having a girl, and I am thankful that I got a beautiful, healthy daughter that has exceeded my expectations in every way. She is a beautiful combination of her daddy and me. She is eight years old at the time of writing this book. She has lived up to her name, meaning "sunshine." She has brought sunshine to everyone who knows her and has been a motivation in my life to be the best I can be. I can see traits in her that I had as a little girl, such as being sensitive to God and caring for her peers. These were things I learned from my parent's love and investment in my life. My hope is she can take what I have learned and run further with it! I am so proud of who she is already as a little girl, and I know she'll influence her generation in a big way!

Love you, Kira! ♥ Mommy

FOREWARD

Warrior Heart is a profound and powerful tool in discovering freedom and fulfillment in your life right now! No matter who you are or where you are in your life journey, freedom awaits you. I am a believer that you can't give away what you don't personally have. As the husband and fan of Katrina's life, I have watched as she has walked through some of the most challenging things in life a person can experience, and yet come out better, stronger, and more loving. I have had a front-row seat to watching her turn tragedy into triumph, pain into power, and fear into fuel as she experienced freedom and liberty. Through her journey to wholeness, God has given Katrina real keys that she shares in this book, which will unlock you where you feel stuck, trapped, or even at the end of your rope. These keys and stories can serve as a prophecy and prediction of great things that you can expect to happen in your own life. She believes freedom from the past, shame, abuse, and fears are what God has for all His people.

This book will be a powerful resource of strength and truth as you go on your journey of freedom from everything that holds you back while finding true fulfillment in your daily life. This book is for everyone ready to break free from the lies, labels, and limits of their past so they can be who they are designed to be. This book will allow you to think about yourself, your value, and the future in a new way. It will restore your ability to dream and bring to life hidden courage and commitment. This tool will cause you to remember who you are and make a meaningful connection to the world around you.

If your joy and freedom have been hindered because of emotional pain, if you have been abused or have suffered from feelings of rejection, I encourage you to read this book. God has inspired Katrina to share the truths she has learned from God's word that set her free. Katrina understands what it means to feel hopeless and unloved. She has put these keys together to give people a solid foundation for people who are ready to let go of their past and move onto the beautiful life God wants them to enjoy.

Based on her own experiences and extensive study, Katrina shares how God's Love will override and overcome the negative results from a negative past and abuse. She shares her insight about

the two types of pain a person must face, the pain of change or the

pain of staying the same. Running from the past does not lead to

healing; in this book, she explains how to move forward through

the pain so you can get better. If you need to let go of the past,

receive healing, and receive an inner strength from God that will

enable you to love yourself, trust again, and enjoy your life, then

this book is for you!

Rex Crain

CONTENTS

Introduction

I believe you have come to this book because you desire change, and you are ready to take charge of your life and future. Deep in your heart, you know that there is more to your life than what you are currently living. I wrote this book with you in mind. I have walked through some difficult and challenging seasons in my journey, and I want to share my story and insights so that you can experience freedom in your soul and live your best life.

You were not born just merely to get by in life and live to feel defeated. God's plan has always been to give you access to live free, clear-minded, healed, and whole. God's description of your life is that He has come to give you abundant life.

I love the word abundant; in Webster's Dictionary, it says, *"present in great quantity; more than adequate; over-sufficient."* God's idea of a good life is that it is more than adequate; it is more than enough. If you're feeling empty about life or life is not how you imagined, your best life is waiting for you. I'm not talking about winning the lottery or becoming rich and famous. I am talking about there is a satisfying life, one that fills your soul! Take this journey

with me on walking into freedom, healing your soul, and living your

best life!

"The thief comes only in order to steal and kill and destroy.

I came that they may have and enjoy life, and have it in

abundance [to the full, till it overflows]." John 10:10 [AMP

Life or Death

I'll never forget the day my life changed forever! It was an ordinary day when my mom took me in for a physical check-up. I was fifteen years old at that time, and the doctor discovered a heart murmur. I ended up being diagnosed with a rare heart disease. The Cardiologists said my aortic root in my heart had ballooned out and was larger than it was supposed to be, and if it kept growing, it would erupt, and I would instantly die.

This was not the news I was expecting to hear from a regular check-up. I was just beginning the process of discovering who I was as a young woman when this news and diagnosis interrupted my life. I was already facing insecurities like everyone else in their teenage years, such as struggling academically and fitting in. For example, I can remember how my teachers made it clear I needed extra help at school, which made me feel that I didn't measure up to others. Not only did I not measure up academically, but now I was told I had a disease. It was a blow to my confidence and outlook in life.

Maybe you could relate, where you have had peers, professionals, or even people close to you that identify or label you based on a flaw or a fact? Maybe like me, your life has been interrupted with a diagnosis of some sort. From our earliest years, we would never imagine disappointment to be at our door. No one ever expects it; it always comes as a shock. But the reality is everyone is faced with unwanted interruptions.

Three years after my diagnosis at eighteen years old, I was told my heart disease had spread to the point that my aortic root was in critical condition, and it was going to erupt any day if I did not get immediate surgery. I had just graduated high school, and my life was ready to begin, or so I thought. I was told that I needed this dangerous and life-threatening surgery if I wanted a chance at life. This was certainly not what I was planning on when I had turned 18 years old and finished high school!

I believed God wanted to do a miracle and even believed He could heal me without doctors, but in my case, He used the doctors.

For three years, I had thoughts that I battled that would come at me; things such as "God was punishing me" or "I may die young." I would often quiet those thoughts by focusing on the truth that's found in God's goodness. I learned to remind myself that God had a good plan for my life and only good thoughts towards me, despite my current challenges. My spiritual life grew as I battled a disease. In my weakness, God became my strength. My understanding and reliance upon God increased, and my fears began to melt away from His love and nearness. I started to become internally strong as His grace carried me.

"My grace is sufficient for you, for my power is made perfect in weakness." 2 Corinthians 12:9

I had so much peace, and I knew God was taking care of me. I could trust Him to the point that I didn't even fear death. I believed my life would not end in early death, and God gave me peace even concerning my eternity. It is a surreal feeling, not being afraid of death. I was at a point that I now needed open-heart surgery. I had to face death in the face, and that is what I did.

5

The Surgeon had told me all the risks and complications. He also mentioned that in 40 years of practicing, he had only done a few cases like mine! He asked me to sign papers the night before the surgery that listed a full page of complications that can end in death. After signing the documents, I was given sleeping pills and instructed to take them later to numb my fears.

That night, I remember taking a bath, and after coming out and wrapping myself in my towel, I looked at my reflection in the mirror and told myself that I would have a new scar after tomorrow. It was an uncomfortable thought. Most girls my age were perfecting their tan and striving for blemish-free skin; I was getting a battle wound.

After I got my pajamas on and climbed into bed, I closed my eyes and asked God for His strength and peace to fill me. I remember feeling calm. I felt a tangible supernatural strength come over me; I read my bible then I dozed off into a deep sleep without taking medicine. I know this is hard to believe, but my rest was so tranquil; it was heavenly and the best sleep of my life! God's love did that for me.

"When you lie down, you will not be afraid; when you lie down, your sleep will be sweet." Proverbs 3:24 [NIV]

The next day, I arrived at the hospital with my parents, who were a great support to me. They stayed with me until I was told to walk into the operating room, where they had me lay on the table. I looked around in the room, which was busy with all the nurses getting everything ready. It was all a little intimating with the equipment and big machines that would preserve my life. I could feel fear trying to creep in, but I focused on how God was with me. A nurse came and explained she would be putting an IV in me that would sedate me for the surgery. At that moment, I knew this was it. I started to confess a scripture I memorized, *"...though I walk through the valley of the shadow of death, I will fear no evil, for You are with me..."* And just like that, I was out.

The surgery was intense and prolonged. It was a six-hour surgery where my heart was stopped for three hours. They drilled through my ribs during this time, cut my aortic root and aortic valve, and replaced it with a titanium one. The Doctors could not believe how bad the condition of my heart was and that I was still alive! They mentioned how paper-thin my aorta was and that it should have erupted already. When they started up my heart to make it pump on its own, it did it right away! It was a miracle, and I had overcome.

The road to recovery was not easy, but I felt proud that I had leaned into God, put on His strength, and conquered what I did. I had chosen not to let the doctors define me as a hopeless case, and instead, decided I was going to be a miracle. I wasn't in denial of what I was facing; I was very aware that it was severe. My focus wasn't on death but was on life! What I discovered is that you can choose life in any situation that feels like death.

"I call heaven and earth as witnesses against you that I have set before you life and death, the blessing and the curse; therefore, you shall choose life so that you may live, you and your descendants." Deuteronomy 30:19 [AMP]

Leaning into my faith, I decided that I wanted to be defined as a miracle even though I was walking through pain. By making this decision, I was able to see a new version of myself and what I could be. I recognized that I could face my giant with a winning mentality. God was with me, and therefore, I could overcome.

In the next pages, you'll discover how I have learned not to be defined by what has happened to me. And I want you to know that change is possible no matter what you have been through, and healing is available.

DAILY PRAYER:

God, I choose life over the areas where I have been hurting and feel dead on the inside. Thank you that your miracles are chasing me down. I know the devil has only come to kill and destroy, but you have come that I may have life. I resist the devil, and I ask you to resurrect my life today. I pray that Your strength would renew me and revive me again today. Thank you that your love is transforming my life. Amen.♥

DAILY CHALLENGE:

Today ask yourself, are you choosing life? If not, where do you need to choose life on purpose? It may be in your health, relationships, or dreams. I encourage you to write it down and rewrite the story of death and appoint life instead.

Labels

It seems like people, parents, and peers are all out to define us from our earliest years. Some of these definitions cripple our potential and limit who we can be. I was fortunate to have parents that spoke faith over my future and potential as I grew up. This helped me to make God's opinion about my life more valuable than the teachers and doctors. Even though these professionals were trying to help me, their diagnosis began to diminish how I saw myself and who I could be. I started to feel that I didn't measure up because of my limitations and the definitions they were now giving me about my future.

As you can see, words are so powerful. Our words and the words of others shape our lives and our experience. Besides, what others speak over us about ourselves often becomes how we see ourselves and the world around us. You may have never had a health challenge, but maybe you are someone who has carried a negative label because of what others have spoken about you or spoken over you.

Negative words are like seeds that we collect from other people's opinions, such as "you are ugly," "you're a loser," or "you're not important." If we allow these words to take root in our hearts and rehearse them in our thoughts, we begin to water them, and they grow. They start to take root in us, and they become our sense of identity of who we are.

Often in life, we don't know why we feel insignificant or insecure. We just think that's who we are. I remember feeling this way and wishing I could have the confidence I saw in others. I thought that's just how they are. I also thought maybe if I didn't have the challenges I was facing, I would feel better about myself. I blamed the way I felt about my life based on my current circumstances and conditions. Maybe you can relate. But I discovered that there are people with much worse circumstances and pain in their lives, yet somehow, they rise above their labels and defy the odds. That's when I learned that a label, much like a deep root in us, can grow, but it can also be weeded out and replaced with good seeds. I realized we oversee what gets planted and unplanted in the garden of our soul.

To grow and flourish into who we were created to be, we need to know our Creator. God planned you before you were born. No one was a mistake. He placed His approval over us before anyone disapproved of us. He has created a purpose and destiny for each person. It's our choice if we want to be merely shaped by other people's suggestions and labels or if we want to pursue a satisfying, healthy life filled with purpose and destiny.

I came to the place in my own experience, where I decided I did not want my life to be known by my limitations or labels others had attached to me. I didn't want to be known as the "girl with the heart disease" or "the girl who wasn't smart." Instead, I shifted my focus from trying to survive a disease to creating a destiny. Instead of seeing my weakness, I turned my focus to God and His miracles. This helped me stand up to fear and defeat. As I did, I began to gain strength and new momentum. It was easy for me to feel scared and feel sorry for myself. It took an intentional decision on my part to be courageous and lean into faith.

Life can be tough! Having a disease is no walk in the park. Despite how I felt, I began to encourage myself by reading stories of people who overcame adversity and the Bible's miracles. As I did, I started to see a different picture. It was a picture of who I was created to be. Lies and self-defeat started to lessen, and courage and purpose began to rise. I was filling my heart with faith that I knew I could face anything with God. I needed God's supernatural strength, and there was no way I could just think myself into positivity. I reminded myself I am not powerless with God; I am an overcomer! This was the wisdom I needed that made me feel stronger and be bigger than a diagnosis even though my physical body was weak. The seeds I had planted in faith were being watered daily, and the roots in my heart were transforming who I was.

You could also be someone who has carried around labels of yourself that are limiting and defeating, such as, "I'm not enough," " I'm a failure," or "I don't measure up." If so, you have probably tried to hide behind a mask, so nobody sees the real you.

No matter what your story is, God does not want to leave you this way. He can make all things new. You can transform. Your history is not your destiny; your identity is your destiny. That's right, your identity and what you believe about yourself is so important; because you will never rise higher than the thoughts and image you carry of yourself. Your thoughts and view of yourself have brought you to where you currently are today, but your thoughts and view of yourself starting today will also take you where you will be in the future. Your future begins now! Today is a great day to create a new identity of who you are going to be.

"If anyone is in Christ, he is a new creation. The old has passed away behold the new has come!" 2 Corinthians 5:17 [NIV]

When you follow your Creator, He transforms you and gives you the power to overcome every label and be the best version of you. I want to share my story so you can learn how to see yourself through the right lenses. Every one of us goes through hard times, but the difficulties do not have to define us.

DAILY PRAYER:

God, today I want to begin the journey to know how You see me. I don't want to be defined by my past, labels, or mistakes. I give those up to you. Make me new and help me to see myself through your eyes. Give me a new understanding of the love you have for me, and let me see who you created me to be. Thank you for your amazing love. Thank you that your love is transforming my life. Amen. ♥

DAILY CHALLENGE:

What are some of the labels that you have carried about yourself and labels that may be holding you back?

Ask God to show you who you are and write it below. His voice is always speaking to your potential!

Look up these Bible verses and write what God says about you:

2 Timothy 1:9:

1 Thessalonians 1:4:

Psalm 17:8:

2 Corinthians 5:17:

Ephesians 1:7:

Psalm 139:14:

Get your fight back!

It would be nice to say that after my heart surgery, everything worked out great in my life, and I never faced a challenge again. That I was unstoppable after defeating my labels, but that is not what took place. I spent a year recovering physically and slowly made progress in living a healthy life again. I began to dream about who I could be and what I could do because I felt I had a whole life ahead of me.

It is interesting when you come face to face with death and conqueror it; you feel you can do anything with God. I always thought that I was going to do something significant that would help people throughout my life. I thought about everything from being a nurse to a missionary. My heart was geared to help those who were suffering or less fortunate.

After many months of gaining my strength back, I decided to pursue a job. My family had known a man who was a pastor and was looking for an assistant. After a couple of conversations, I got the job. My family and I did not know that he was a predator who would use his position of power to take advantage of women. Within a couple of weeks, I was in a scary situation where I was raped. This never even crossed my mind that someone in this type of position could do this to me and others; it was a frightening and horrific thing that happened. Never in a million years could I imagine that this would happen to me, especially after just going through a life-threatening surgery.

Immediately I was faced with a whole new set of challenges. I felt so much shame and blamed myself; I had been violated and tainted. I had just defeated the labels and overcome the odds of heart disease, and now here I was victimized and violated by an evil person who abused my trust. Questions began to run through my mind, "where do I go?" and "what do I do" I courageously made the decisions in the face of fear to call the police and give a report about the abuse and evil that had just been done. Immediately, despite the sense of victory I had experienced only a couple of months previously, I no longer felt like a miracle.

This sent me down on a destructive emotional spiral that manifested into depression and bulimia. I started battling with the lie that something was wrong with me, and that is why all this had happened. The feelings of shame and guilt began to slowly take over my mind, and I felt like my life was ruined. I was now a hostage, broken, and stuck in a dark place that was much deeper than hearing the diagnosis that I had heart disease; it was a profound violation of my soul.

I felt distant from God because I carried so much shame. I felt unworthy. Brene Brown, a shame researcher, describes shame well,

"The intensely painful feeling or experience of believing that we are flawed and therefore unworthy of love and belonging - something we've experienced, done, or failed to do makes us unworthy of connection."

This is how I felt; shame made me feel disconnected. I fell deeper into shame because now I had an eating disorder I had to hide.

I let so many lies fill my mind that I began to lose sight of who I was. My dream life of living happily ever after began to crumble and collapse because of the pain that was happening. It made no sense. I remember going to the doctor because I thought something must be wrong in my body; I had not felt this way before.

I soon discovered this wasn't a physical alignment but a mental and emotional pain called depression. I spent months asking God to remove my pain and suffering. The lies started to get out of control, and I began to believe if I could control my body size and weight, maybe I would feel better. I was looking for a superficial way to fix how I felt in my soul. When I ate, I felt terrible, and then I would throw up. This lie created a new normal in my life where I would plan my days around eating and purging. I would feel such extreme shame, so I made sure I hid this secret addiction. I believed that if I could get down to my ideal size, my life would be better, and I would feel better. I was blinded to the truth by believing these lies and acting on them, but they were only hurting me greater.

After a year into this deep, awful cycle, my parents, brother, and sister noticed that I was struggling with a real problem. They lovingly confronted me, and at first, I denied it; but their words were real, and I knew I needed help. What my family said to me aided me in acknowledging that I needed help and that I had a real problem. It takes courage to say you need help; just admitting it can be challenging, but there is so much freedom in the act of recognizing that you can't keep living the same way anymore. Shame will seek to hold us from revealing the truth, but God said there is freedom when we walk towards the truth. The truth is what sets us free. Lies are what will hold us down and keep us in secret. It takes courage to tell someone you need help.

I found that God is happy and pleased when we take this step because it opens the door to real healing and restoration. Before I decided to acknowledge and admit I had a problem, I talked myself out of it many times. I felt shame, and I was too embarrassed about who I had become. When I realized I didn't want to live this way anymore, I mustered the courage to face the truth in the open. There's a huge load that comes off just by facing reality, especially with an addiction, and saying these three words, "I need help."

The road to getting better seemed like an uphill battle. Once again, I thought it would be too hard, but I found that the pain of staying the same was higher than the pain of fighting for freedom. I have learned God has empowered us to do hard things!

Fighting off the lies and walking into the truth was my road to recovery. During this time, I had a breakthrough when I felt the depression start to lift, and hope began to fill my soul. God had shown me something powerful; He showed me that the person who had done this evil to me had touched my body, but they had no access to my heart without my permission. I oversaw what I let in my heart, and no one else has that power over me. This was the first time I could distinguish what had happened to me and who I was. I found people can do evil to me, but they don't have power over me. God gives us control over what we keep in our hearts, and evil acts do not need to live in us or have power over us.

"Don't be afraid of those who want to kill your body; they cannot touch your soul." Mathew 10:28. [NLT]

This verse spoke to me; it tells me that I am more than my body. Evil had victimized me, but I didn't have to stay a victim in my mind. Once I realized that God gave me the power to choose life, I decided to stand up for my life and fight; I no longer had to live in brokenness and darkness.

I decided to get aggressive with my beliefs and break free from my mental torment. I acknowledged my soul was hurting, and I decided that I wanted to do the work to heal. I fought for my life again, but this time for my emotional and mental freedom. I realized that no one could do it for me; there would be no magic pill. I was the only one who could choose freedom and life for myself, and that is what I did.

Can I tell you something I wish someone had told me? It was very hard at first, and I thought it would take years to fix my soul, but God helped me process the pain and find real healing. He even sped up my healing! This was so powerful because if I tried to do it on my strength, I could spend my whole life fighting the same soul battles. God is ready to help in our time of need, and he wants us to live in freedom more than we do.

It wasn't long before I found that I began to have more happy days than sad days after a few months with God. I was able to resist the desire to purge, and I started feeling better about myself. I am so glad that I pushed through the pain and did what I could to get better every day. The freedom you feel on the other side cannot compare to some of the hard things you have to do to get there. God promises in His word to "work all things together for our good." When you give Him your pain, He will turn it around.

DAILY PRAYER:

Jesus, thank you for the price you paid for my freedom. I want to experience your freedom in new ways. You said where the Spirit of the Lord is that there is freedom. I ask that you break oppression and any addictions from my life. Help me to exchange my defeat for your victory. I surrender anything that's holding me back from your freedom. I trust you, and thank you that your love is transforming my life. Amen.♥

DAILY CHALLENGE:

Read this verse below and meditate on how it can change your life. Write your thoughts on what comes to mind when you read these verses:

> *"Are you tired? Worn out? Burned out on religion? Come to me. Get away with Me, and you'll recover your life. I'll show you how to take a real rest. Walk with me and work with me - watch how I do it. Learn the unforced rhythms of grace. I won't lay anything heavy or ill-fitting on you. Keep company with Me, and you'll learn to live freely and lightly."* Matthew 11:28-30 [MSG]

4

Take Back Your Power

Have you ever heard of someone doing something great, and they achieved it by feeling sorry for themselves? No! I haven't either. The people that inspire us had every reason to give up facing obstacles and challenges but decided they would not stay stuck being a victim. The most inspiring stories among us are those born with disadvantages or terrible odds yet pushed past the emotional and physical limits of their conditions by creating something amazing with their life!

God wants to help each of us move forward past the circumstances, weakness, and pain we currently find ourselves facing. He desires that all our lives be special; it is not where we start but where we end. To end well and create a great life, we must be willing to shake off self-pity and feeling sorry for ourselves.

Deciding not to settle in self-pity and victimhood is one of the essential steps towards freedom that you can take. Choosing to be committed to a breakthrough allows you to reclaim the power you have been giving away and decide who you will be and what you will do. God is near a broken heart; He sympathizes with our pain and is gentle and loving. Sometimes we just need to soak in His love to get the strength to heal. There is a point in your healing that you cannot stay a victim anymore if you want to move on. If you're going to be set free, you must embrace the truth.

Throughout the Bible, God calls us "victors," not "victims." And those who overcame crazy circumstances saw that they could defy the odds and overcome with God. If you keep a victim mentality, you will become crippled in life.

Why will you become crippled in life if you keep a victim mentality? Because when you are a victim, you feel pity for yourself. You believe you have suffered more than is fair or reasonable; you complain about why your life is the way it is or blame events, others, yourself, or even God for your current reality. There are many cases like mine; you became the victim of other's ugly choices. You may say, "If this person didn't hurt me, I wouldn't be the way I am." or, "If only I didn't grow up the way I did, I wouldn't be the way I am." You could blame your life on your childhood or not having what others have. There are so many ways we can reason our "victimhood." When you are a victim, you can develop negative traits like being controlling, manipulative, fearful, closed off, insecure, and harsh. It can make it hard for others to get along with you.

It is hard to believe in a promising future when you are stuck in pity. You look for others to make things happen for your future instead of taking charge of your future. Weeds grow automatically, but flowers take work and effort. Look at life's inevitable hardships to grow stronger and become better. Some people have gotten used to feeling sorry for themselves, throwing pity parties, and inviting others to join in: "You poor thing! You have been through so much!"

Face it, we all enjoy a little pity occasionally. Still, if it becomes a lifestyle, you start giving yourself reasons to stay the same by using the defense mechanisms of complaining and blaming. These self-defeating enemies keep you locked into an old life and situation, but once you determine that you are ready to give up all your victim stories of why you can't, why you haven't, etc., you can move towards healing and strength!

"But You, O Lord, are a shield for me, my glory and the One who lifts up my head." Psalm 3:3 [NKJ].

God wants us to lift our heads, find our backbone, face our pain, and begin to heal. Throughout the Scripture, He often talks about identity and how we see, perceive, and relate to ourselves. The words He uses to describe us are often powerful words such as bold, strong, courageous, loved, and generous. I have noticed that whenever He references someone's weakness, He shifts the conversation to what His strength can provide. *"...Let the weak say, ' I am strong."* Joel 3:10

So how can you become strong if you feel weak? First, you must know that God will never waste your pain! You can only sit in self-pity for so long, and at some point, you must make the decision that you want to lean into God's strength. You need to decide to be strong and to be strong, I mean, you should discover what God says about you and make that your new reference point.

You cannot expect to build muscles and strength without lifting weights, the same way you will not know God's strength without building it inside you. There are challenging times when you call on Him; you receive immediate strength for the situation like I did while facing my heart surgery. If you want power in your everyday life, you need to be connected to the source of life to draw strength. The wisdom of God will always lead you to a place of wholeness and victory in your heart and mind. I made a power move for my life when I chose not to be defined by what had happened to me. I didn't want to be a victim of my circumstance anymore. This was living courageous, and it's not easy by any means, but anyone who ever did anything significant in life challenged themselves and overcame their obstacles. I did not want to be known and defined by my circumstances, but by my courage. I can relate to those who have decided to do the same thing in their life.

The story of Bethany Hamilton inspires me. She is an American professional surfer who survived a vicious shark attack that bit off her left arm. You might have heard of her story in the last couple of years. She had every reason to spend the rest of her life, feeling sorry for herself by reliving the trauma and giving up on her dreams. The very thing she loved seemed to be taken away from her because of the loss of her arm. That was no minor hurdle to move past, and it was a big deal.

Her story is so compelling because she did not let her limitations stop her. After only a month of recovering, she went back into the ocean to face her fears. God gave her the strength, and she taught herself how to surf again, this time using one arm. What is powerful is that she did not let her fears hold her back; instead, she chose to use courage to rise above her circumstance. She went on to win surfing championships against people who had both their arms.

Her story of courage caught the attention of producers in Hollywood. They made an inspiring movie about her life that challenges millions of people everywhere from every walk of life to not give up on their dreams, even when there are setbacks, adversities, and limitations. Today, Bethany is happily married and has children. She uses her story and platform to be a great role model to inspire the impossible. Her story is encouraging because she did not let what happened to her define who she could become.

Many people have been a victim of unfortunate events like myself or Bethany. But when you hold onto a victim mentality, you can never walk into who you are destined to be. Today you can say you don't want to carry this label anymore! Be bold and courageous, and decide you want to grow and break free from this mindset. I encourage you to remind yourself that you are not powerless, and you can overcome. Make this confession today, and allow your life to go from strength to strength!

DAILY PRAYER:

God, today I want to give up my victim status. I don't want to let what's happened in my life define me. I want your truth to define me. Help me to discard feeling sorry for myself and powerless. Help me to move towards the overcoming life You've promised me. I want to experience your strength in new ways. Thank you that your love is transforming my life. Amen. ♥

DAILY CHALLENGE:

Make this confession:

"Today, with God's help, I choose to let go of any victim status I have held on to. This limiting belief will not dictate my life any longer. I choose to take back my power and own the fact that God has made me overcome in life. I am more than an overcomer with Jesus, and this is the posture I see my life with."

Write down how this confession is changing your life!

Believe Again

Zechariah 9:12 says, *"Return to your stronghold, O prisoners of hope; today I declare that I will restore to you double."*

If you don't have hope, you don't have life. If you don't feel you have hope and a purpose, you start to die on the inside. Sometimes through disappointments, we decide to settle in life, and we stop expecting much. I know that has happened in my life. When I was expecting things to turn out one way and then, it did not happen for whatever reason. Yet, hope is so essential to have; it is an expectation that something good can happen to us, no matter what is taking place in our life.

"Hope deferred makes the heart sick, but a sudden good break turns life around." Proverbs 13:12 [NIV]

Today can be a sudden good break for you! Where hope can fill your heart again, and you can see things turn around in your life. God wants each of us to hold onto hope for our future, even if things are difficult in our present. Everyone needs hope to pursue a future; God placed this longing in us. Wrong thinking tries to trick you into thinking there is no hope for you. It wants you to believe that you have blown it too many times, or that you will never meet the right partner, that life will never get better, or you'll never live the life of your dreams. The truth is you have not lived your best day yet!

One amazing story of a person who did not lose hope and pursued a good future, we can all agree we are thankful for, is Walt Disney. Disney dreamed of being an artist as a young man. When he told his parents of his dream, they discouraged him and wanted him to join the family business making jam. He pursued his dreams of being an artist anyway.

At twenty-two years old, he was fired from one of his first animation jobs at a newspaper because his editor felt that he " lacked imagination and had no good ideas." That wasn't the last of his setbacks! Disney then acquired an animation studio that he later drove into bankruptcy. Walt Disney's hope for a bright future was not moved by his family's discouragement, his boss ' s negativity, nor his business going under. He kept pursuing what he loved!

He had many challenges along the way, and it has been stated that Disney was turned down 302 times before finally getting financing for his dream of creating Walt Disney World! Millions of people are thankful for Disney not giving up and looking to his future with hope and expectancy of what can be.

"Don't let your fears take the place of your dreams." Walt Disney

This is the time for you to activate the power of hope. A good starting point is to ask yourself, "Are you looking for and believing for the best?" or "Are you expecting to recycle the past, be disappointed again, and things to remain the same?" If you choose to hope, you must see as I did that negativity will have to go; hope and cynicism cannot coexist.

A critical spirit and a complaining attitude will stop hope from operating. Once you start getting critical in your mind about where you are or what you are going through, you begin to feel burdened, tired, or depressed. The attitude of "what I am doing makes no difference" can bring the same results. These attitudes keep you focused on the wrong thing and steals a life full of expectancy.

You may have endured pain, disappointments, loss, and it has made you feel hopeless. You could think that nothing good works out in your life so, why expect anything good in the future? When you give in to this thinking, your mind becomes clouded by what you are going through. This is a trap, and you can take charge of the feeling of hopelessness; it does not have to dominate you. You are not what you feel, but you are what you decide.

When you choose to believe that your future will be better than where you have been, hope will begin to drive out the doubt and despair you feel. Hope is a powerful force. That is why I want to challenge you to hold onto it purposely. Why? Because it influences your mind, your mood, and your outlook. Hope builds us up as we wait on God; it believes that all things are possible with God. Even when things seem the darkest and the most difficult, the power of hope in the goodness of God will release strength for you to rise above.

When you are focused on a good future, you also produce joy! The Bible says that the joy of the Lord is our strength. When I think of a joyful person, I think of a thankful person. One way to activate hope is to think of all the reasons you can be grateful. This makes you remember the victories you had in your past, which will give you an expectation of what can happen in your future. When you focus on what you still have rather than what you have lost, your attitude changes, hope begins to grow.

> *"For I know the plans I have for you," declares the Lord, "plans to prosper you and not to harm you, plans to give you hope and a future."* Jeremiah 29:11 [NIV]

DAILY PRAYER:

God, I ask that you fill me with new levels of hope for my life today. Remove the clouds of disappointment and give me expectancy as I had as a kid. Fill me with childlike faith, wonder, and joy. Thank you that the joy of the Lord is my strength. Let me experience this strength in my life. Let me laugh today! Thank you that your love is transforming my life. Amen. ♥

DAILY CHALLENGE:

I want you to notice how you can change your emotional state as you make a committed decision to focus on all the good in your life. Hope is available!

What are you grateful and hopeful for in your life right now?

What about that makes you grateful and hopeful?

How does this make you feel?

6

The Power of Vision

Hellen Keller, who was a famous blind author, was once asked, "What is worse than being born blind?" Her response was inspiring, "Having sight with no vision." She recognized the power of vision. Vision brings strength in our lives, whether we realize it or not. We move toward what we see in our minds. If what we see is limited to the past, we will find ourselves reliving and recycling old experiences that leave us disappointed and defeated. The Bible speaks about the creative force of vision in our lives when it says, "*Where there is no vision, people perish.*"[Proverbs 29:18, KJV] In another translation, it says, *"If people can't see what God is doing, they stumble all over themselves; But when they attend to what he reveals, they are most blessed.."* [MSG] This is an accurate picture of us when we lack vision for who we can become, what we can do, and what we can experience in our future. If we don't have a vision for our future, we will find it easy to return to our past.

When we get a new vision in our hearts, something happens on the inside of us. Hope and motivation begin to move us from the state we are in into a future state that promises victory. Vision will allow you to move beyond the pain of the past to the hope of a future. I discovered that once I started developing an idea for my future, the shackles of what once held me started falling off. I believe the same thing will happen for you today.

The vision that I started developing began as I looked to God's Word and not my circumstances. I had to make a conscious choice to look away from my surroundings to see something new. Wherever you find yourself today, there is hope because His Word is a light to your path. As you open His Word and allow it to speak to you, it will begin to paint a picture of a life and future you never thought possible.

One of the most empowering things I did was to look at models that could motivate me. I wanted to find someone who had faced challenges but found a way to turn their tragedy into triumph and pain into power. I believe success leaves clues. Maybe that is why the Bible gives us so many personal examples of people who had rough beginnings and unfortunate circumstances. Through

God's grace and Word, these same people were able to turn things around. In the modern world, a woman that has stood out to me is Joyce Meyers. She is an accomplished writer with over fifty books in print, and I discovered her work through one of them. What helped me was the feeling that she understood the heartache and pain I was experiencing. Yet, she did not stay there but found the courage to stand up and fight for her freedom after being molested, abandoned, and rejected.

She said something that stood out to me as I read her story. She stated that with the work she invested in becoming the person she is today, "it seems as if the old person had never even existed." This spoke to me. I knew that if I was willing to work with God and invest in myself, I could feel the same way. That gave my heart so much confidence and hope!

God has since removed the pain of what I walked through to the point that it feels like a different person and different life when I think back. The sting of my past is so far removed that even when I talk of it to help others, it is as though it wasn't my story. God truly can make things new; I believe He wants to do that in your life right now. He doesn't want to cover something up with a band-aid, but He wants to heal you at the core of who you are so you can find freedom and enjoy who He made you be.

> *"See, I am doing a new thing! Now it springs up; do you not perceive it? I am making a way in the wilderness and streams in the wasteland."* Isaiah 43:18-19 [NIV]

When we feel like we have been in a wasteland or wilderness, God encourages us not to look at the current situation as permanent but as a temporary place to pass through. He says He will do a new thing. If you are in a wasteland, ask God what He wants to do in your life? Maybe you desire a calm and undisturbed mind free from anxiety, or perhaps you just want to feel innocence again or find joy. Whatever it is, God is ready to heal your soul and pour his rain over your life so that new things can grow. Decide today that your life must change!

Vision not only gives us hope to pull us into the future, but it directs and focuses our lives on what matters most. When you can see or envision a better, happier, and more significant future, you are more likely to make the necessary changes to reach that kind of life. God gives us a vision in His word for what our lives can be. I'd like to ask you a personal question for a moment: What is it that you would like to see in your future? If you were to write what an extraordinary and abundant life looked like, what would you say, or how would you describe it? What are the consistent emotions you want to feel? Where would you like to make a difference, and how?

Whatever the vision is, you need to imagine that if you don't go after it, what would it cost you? I have asked myself this question on many occasions because I want to see what cost it will be to me if I stay where I am without changing and going after my future. And I want to take back ownership and responsibility in my life; I don't want just to be a passive bystander. After you decide what you want to become and what results you are committed to, one of the practical and tactical things is to write it down where you can consistently see and reference them. Make your atmosphere worthy of your attention.

The reality is that you will arrive somewhere in the next six months, whether it is a short-term goal or a long-term commitment. If you don't plan where you will arrive, you will be stuck in the same place. I hope that lights a fire in you that something must change!

A powerful tool I used when I decided to end up somewhere on purpose was to make a list of confessions about who I was going to become. To be real with you, this is still a powerful tool I use daily. It allows me to live in the emotional freedom God has for me. When I started, I would find myself revisiting these confessions three or more times a day. I wrote down the truth to defeat the lies. The lies try to destroy the vision I am committed to seeing through.

Some of these confessions are:

+ I am a beautiful and confident woman who God loves.
+ My confidence comes from who God says I am, not my body or my peers.
+ I am healthy and walk in freedom.
+ God says I am worthy, lovable, and good things are coming my way.
+ I am forgiven and am more than a conqueror over guilt, shame, and fear.

I would find Bible verses to fill my mind with truth to focus on where I was going. The more I spoke these confessions, the more my emotional experience began to change. I started to see my vision more clearly. I know we all want to start viewing everything clearly, but I found it does not work that way. I followed God's example; He spoke light when there was darkness and fullness when there was emptiness. The amazing thing was that copying His model began to replace the void with fullness and dark with light and vision.

"A person has joy by the answer of their mouth." Proverbs 15:23 [NKJV]

"My innermost being rejoices when my lips speak right things." Proverbs 23:16 [NKJV]

" ...your faith may become effective through the knowledge of every good thing which is in you..." Philemon 1:6 [NAS]

I can honestly say, I did not always feel what I was confessing, but that's okay because our feelings will catch up to our confessions. Doctor Caroline Leaf, who is a brain expert and specialist, says that after twenty-one days of confessing the truth, you begin to create brand new brain pathways. Neurons start firing that were not firing before. No wonder it is said that it takes twenty-one days to form a new habit. That's how long it takes for the brain to agree with your new habit.

The good news is that with God, all things are possible! Even your body can discover health when you speak life over it. Sometimes the miracle you are seeking does not happen in an instant, but God's Word in our mouths will allow us to go beyond the barriers we feel and discover a life of miracles.

DAILY PRAYER:

God, I ask that you open my eyes to your vision for my life. Where depression, anxiety, or fear have crippled me and stopped my vision, I ask that You give me healing in a new way. Help me to confess and believe in a good future. Help my confessions line up with your visions and plans for my life. Thank you that your love is transforming my life. Amen.♥

DAILY CHALLENGE:

What are some confessions you can speak over your life? Write them down and read them out loud to yourself!

222

2222222222

7

Your Mind is a Weapon

One of the simplest yet profound concepts I have learned was that I need to think about what I am thinking. This sounds silly at first, but are you aware of what thoughts fill your head daily? I realized I felt so poorly of myself when I battled an eating disorder. During this struggle, I began to realize I had no control over my thought life. I would simply entertain any thought that came into my head. Does that sound familiar? For me, it was a consistent stream of tormenting thoughts like, "I don't care to live anymore." "I was a helpless case," and then at other times, it was, "I am ugly." I felt out of control and overwhelmed, even if there wasn't a lot going on in my life. It was because my thoughts were out of control and suppressing me. I felt terrible about myself, and I had a lingering depressive cloud over my head.

When you feel bad about yourself, it is easy to become self-absorbed and get used to feeling bad. The enemy of our life tries to defeat us in our thought life. If he can get you to believe lies about yourself, you lose your power and hope. The devil does have the ability but no authority over you unless you permit him by believing in his lies. The way to allow him is through making agreements with a distortion about yourself.

Satan wants you to be so focused on your problems, mistakes and hurts that you don't have the energy or time to pursue your destiny and help others. The Bible says your enemy, the Devil, is an accuser. He likes to accuse you of your failures, lies, and limiting beliefs. Next time you find yourself in self-pity, rehearsing all the reasons why your life's awful or even why you think you are terrible, remember you are allowing the enemy to have access to you.

When you make a lifestyle of believing his lies, you create strongholds in your mind. These are limiting beliefs and thoughts that you think are real. For example, you might not think you are good enough; this is a type of stronghold in your mind. The way to disempower and defeat the lies is to learn to take these negative thoughts captive and choose to think the right thoughts.

"For though we walk in the flesh, we do not war according to the flesh. For the weapons of our warfare are not carnal

but mighty in God for pulling down strongholds casting

down arguments and every high thing that exalts itself

against the knowledge of God, bringing every thought into

captivity to the obedience of Christ."

2 Corinthians 10:3-6 [NKJV]

Self-sabotaging thoughts and limiting beliefs are arguments that exalt themselves against the knowledge of God. The Bible makes it clear just how much power is in our thought life. We are to bring every thought to line up with Christ's. It helps to see that sometimes the war in our head is a spiritual war. If you want to measure your spiritual warfare meter, ask yourself, "does my thought life line up with God's thought life for me?" Are you being defeated in your thought life because you are ruled by how you feel? Do you let negative thoughts run out of control? If you want to grow spiritually, pay attention to what you are thinking!

God's desire and plan is for us to live in freedom; He cares about what we think. We must take inventory of our thought life and use the truth to transform and refresh our minds. At first, this might seem overwhelming because it takes time to break down lies. Over time it becomes a habit and produces so much peace in your mind that it becomes easy. I realized my thoughts were sabotaging me and negatively affecting the way I felt. Reversing my thinking and how I felt seemed like it would take years, but I decided it didn't matter because I wanted to act and experience freedom.

Every day you need to pay attention to your thoughts. You can't let thoughts that are hurting you and your mind just pass. You may even need to talk to someone to help you discover the reoccurring thoughts that are sabotaging and holding you back. Counselors, or people who love you, can be a real help to you when you reach out. The key is to confront the negative thoughts by learning to speak the truth into the lies.

For instance, I remember I would tell myself in many different ways, " I don't measure up, and everyone knows." I would revisit these thoughts daily, to the point I didn't like going out because I was self-absorbed in my insecurity and shame. I was so fragile that I thought many times if a stranger was laughing in my direction, they were laughing at me. My anxious thoughts were tormenting me, not even to go out. Until someone helped me realize people are not that focused on me, and it was just a stupid lie I was believing. Every time I was in public when someone looked at me funny, I had to say, "they are not focusing on me. I am good enough, confident, and a lovable person." I began to recognize that when I felt poorly, my thoughts made me feel down.

Other times when I felt I was starting to feel sorry for myself, I took a proactive approach by reading books and listening to messages that would speak life in me. I wouldn't let my mind play re-runs of how horrible my life had become. I would call someone, re-direct my thoughts, journal positive confessions, pray, listen to uplifting worship music, and purposefully avoid negative news on social media, tv, etc. It was hard at first to get a handle on my negativity, but I was determined to rule my mind and brainwash myself with the truth of who I was!

> *"Do not conform to the pattern of this world, but be trans-formed by the renewing of your mind. Then you will be able to test and approve what God's will is - His good, pleasing, and perfect will."* Romans 12:2 [NIV]

God helped me do this and walk this process out with grace. The word "transformed" here in the Greek language means "metamorphosis" (changing from one form to another). This means that changing your thought life does not happen overnight. It is a process and takes time to learn how to think right, but it is well worth it!

When you change your thought life, you will begin to experience real peace, to the point it doesn't even make sense at times why you have peace. Jesus peace settles you, it's true, lasting inner peace and it's unaffected by outward circumstances. When you learn to lean into this peace and not your emotions your mind gets renewed. You learn to control your thoughts, give your worries to God and not be a victim to whatever pops into your head. You lead your mind and are in control.

"Be anxious for nothing, but in everything by prayer and supplication, with thanksgiving, let your requests be made known to God; and the peace of God, which surpasses all understanding, will guard your hearts and minds through Christ Jesus. Finally, brethren, whatever things are true, whatever things are noble, whatever things are just, whatever things are pure, whatever things are lovely, whatever things are of good report, if there is any virtue and if there is anything praiseworthy - meditate on these

things. The things which you learned and received and heard and saw in me, these do, and the God of peace will be with you." Philippians 4:6-9 [NIV]

DAILY PRAYER:

God, today give me the power to take charge of my thought life. I need your grace to help me think right and discard what's hurting me. Show me how to renew my mind through Your Word. Give me revelation and knowledge that I can break any thought patterns that are oppressing me. Nothing is too hard with you! I can do all things through you, God; You strengthen me. Thank you that Your love is transforming my life. Amen. ♥

DAILY CHALLENGE:

Think about this last week and ask yourself if you spent time in a mental battle with oppressing thoughts? Write them down and speak the truth to those lies. If you need help seeing the truth, ask someone who can help you see the truth in those lies. Make sure you write the truth down, so you can go back to it and remind yourself. Whenever those thoughts come up again, you must go back to the truth. I would encourage you to read the truth daily, so the information becomes your revelation and becomes a part of you.

Accepting Yourself

I spent many days believing the lie that if I could just have the perfect body, I would be enough and accept myself. I had struggled with an eating disorder that had become my master and the way of accepting myself. In my deception, I thought a perfect body would equate to love and acceptance. I got to 98 pounds and still never felt good enough.

On the other side of that lie, I can say the only way to feel comfortable in your skin and feel accepted truly, is by knowing your Creator loves and accepts you just the way you are. When we accept ourselves because God accepts us, we don't have to feel negative emotions towards ourselves, leading to self-destructive behaviors and habits.

Have you noticed that when you don't like yourself, it's because you carry beliefs that something is wrong with you? When you think something is wrong with you, you never feel good enough. You will work hard to overcompensate in other areas of your life to mask feelings of not being enough. You will try to feel good enough through people's approval, a career, perfectionism, body image, status, or false success. You will spend your life on a chase for approval.

The good news is this chase can end when you discover that God accepts your faults, flaws and all; and because He accepts you, you can accept yourself. Choosing this truth is liberating because when you can accept what God accepts, it empowers you to forgive yourself for not being perfect. When you choose God's truth, it also enables you to love yourself healthily.

You can accept yourself because God accepts you; He made you so He could love you! This is a truth to build your life upon. God did not need you. He was not lonely. He made you so that you could share His love. You're not an accident; you're the result of an intentional Creator who wanted you. Your parents may not have wanted or planned you, but God did! The reality is, the only reason that you are alive and breathing at this moment is because He wills you exist.

"Your eyes saw my substance, being yet unformed. And in Your book, they all were written, the days fashioned for me when as yet there were none of them. How precious also are Your thoughts to me, O God! How great is the sum of them! If I should count them, they would be more in number than the sand; When I awake, I am still with You."
Psalms 139:16-18 [KJV]

I love this verse because it gives a beautiful picture of God's loving thoughts towards us. We can't even count how great they are since they are more than all the sand on the beach. Next time you go to the beach, think about that as you hold a handful of sand. God cannot help but lavish His love on us, and when you know God accepts you, you can accept yourself.

We all have flaws and things we wish we could change about ourselves, but God designed us perfectly. He imagined us before we came to the planet, and He made His mind up about us to love us even if we reject Him. You and I are the focus of His love. His Word says, "Christ died for us while we were yet sinners." This is unconditional love! If God wanted to accept us while we rejected Him, why is it so hard to accept ourselves even when we know God?

I think most of us try to relate to God's love, like human love. Often, human love and even those close to us can reject us if we are not perfect or do everything right. Many feel they must earn approval from others for what they do, not just being loved for who they are. People can love us when we do the right things and then leave us if we don't measure up to their standard later on. We can put these standards on ourselves and internally reject ourselves when we are not the right size, didn't say the right thing, messed up that day, etc. The enemy of our lives works hard to get us to focus on what is wrong instead of what is right. Whatever you focus on grows, and if you continuously see yourself as "wrong," you will feel wrong and not approve of yourself. If you focus on God's unconditional love and that He loves us the same on our worst day as He does on our best day, this love changes how we treat ourselves. The devil works diligently to get us to reject and devalue ourselves in our minds. He knows that what we don't value, we will eventually violate.

We must see ourselves through the lens of God's love. Liking yourself doesn't mean you are a prideful person; it merely means you accept yourself as the person God created you to be. Even if you are not where you want to be in life, no one is perfect, and we are all growing. While we are on this earth, each one of us can improve ourselves and our life. Accepting ourselves as God's creation is essential to our progress in becoming a healthy person. God loves you unconditionally all the time. You're a unique individual with your own set of strengths and weaknesses. And even though you've made mistakes in the past (and will in the future), you can move on and learn to like yourself.

The root of accepting yourself is knowing that you are approved unconditionally by God. If you have believed differently about Him, think about one of your best moments where you felt like you deserved God's love, then compare it to one of your least proud moments. Those same moments never affected God's love towards you. Even on your darkest day where God didn't like what you did, He still loved you as deeply as he did on your best day, where you represented Him well. It's a crazy concept because we have a hard time with this kind of love, but

God is love, and this revelation can change your life!

DAILY PRAYER:

God, today I give up the pressure of looking for people's approval, and I want my life secure in Your approval of me. Thank You for loving me the same on my worst days as on my best day. Let new depths of Your love deliver me from other's acceptance. Holy Spirit, teach me to hear what You are speaking over me more than any other voice. Thank You that Your love is transforming my life. Amen. ♥

DAILY CHALLENGE:

Today make two lists and answer these questions thoughtfully:
1.   What do <u>you see</u> when you look in the mirror?

2.What do you think <u>God sees</u> when He looks at you?

If you have drastic answers between the two questions, take time to study God's thoughts for your life. Read the Bible with His eyes of love towards you. When you get a revelation of His love, you can change how you see yourself.

9

Forgive Yourself

To live in freedom and accept who you are, you must be willing to forgive yourself. Remember that nothing surprises God. He knew what He was getting when He chose to enter a relationship with you. The last thing He wants for us is to be separated from Him by guilt and condemnation. Guilt is a feeling which can let us know we did something wrong, but we are not to stay living in guilt. Guilt makes us obsessed with rehearsing our failures and mistakes over and over in our minds. And it starts to affect who we are. God's plan is not for us to carry regret and guilt.

"Therefore, there is now no condemnation for those who are in Christ Jesus, because through Christ Jesus the law of the Spirit who gives life has set you free from the law of sin and death." Romans 8:1-2 [NIV]

When Jesus died for our sins, He took away the punishment of guilt held against us, so we don't have to carry it. He made a way out, so we don't get what we deserve when we mess up. Sometimes we deal with consequences from our mistakes and failures, but God does not want us to live in condemnation and hate towards ourselves. When we accept Christ in our life, He makes us new.

> *"Therefore, if anyone is in Christ, he is a new creation; old things have passed away; behold, all things have become new."* 2 Corinthians 5:17 [NKJV]

> *"For you, Lord, are good, and ready to forgive, and abundant mercy to all those who call upon you."* Psalm 86:5 [NKJV]

Does that sound like God is holding our past against us? When we choose life with Jesus, He says that everything we are not proud of and feel guilty for He remembers it no more. You are not a failure, a sinner, or defined by your worst day; through Jesus, all things become new. I am sure, like me, your feelings have tried to convince you that you are not worthy, but we must recognize that thought is to keep us from freeing our minds. God's Word tells us that Jesus paid the price for the forgiveness of our sins and removed our guilt.

I have an amazing friend named Jessica; she is a beautiful example of receiving God's love for her life. Jessica spent many years seeing herself being unworthy. She always carried shame and unforgiveness towards herself. She went through much of her life having a poor self-image of herself. As a teenager, she attracted the wrong men who abused her physically and emotionally. She would be battered and beat up but didn't have the strength to leave. She was hurting and broken.

When she became a young woman, she found herself pregnant from a guy she barely knew. Although being pregnant was a shock, she made the brave choice to keep her baby. When her baby was born, she fell in love with her beautiful daughter, Jayda. She was perfect in Jessica's eyes and gave her a sense of purpose for her soul. As Jess cared for and loved her daughter, she noticed that her baby struggled with some abnormalities. It wasn't long after that she discovered those abnormalities were very serious. This news brought a whole new reality that would rock her world.

Not only was she a young single mother, which being a new mom is challenging, but the doctors discovered her precious baby was born both blind and disabled. Her baby was diagnosed with a life-threatening condition, which led to many hospitalizations and her daughter being in and out of ICU. The pain of life began to be too much to carry as she watched her baby suffer.

Looking for a way to numb her reality, she became addicted to medicating herself. Jessica loved her daughter and was a good mom, but she couldn't handle watching her suffer and fight for her life daily. After many years of watching her daughter suffer, my friend decided life was not worth living. Her life, in her eyes, was a pile of ashes full of pain, shame, and despair. With little hope, she tried to end her life. This occurred several times without success – but God was just waiting to love her!

I had been a friend to her over the years, continually loving her and letting her know that God had good plans for her life. Jessica was always open to hearing about God, but she wasn't ready to surrender until one day. This day wasn't much different than other days that my husband and I met her for dinner. Before she met with us, she had taken too much medication to numb herself. As we sat down for dinner and began to have a conversation, she had difficulty staying awake and talking. She was very ill, and we asked if we could bring her to our car, to which she agreed.

My husband (without drawing a lot of attention to the scene to protect her) carried her to our car, where she had a hard time breathing and gasping for air. We were close to the hospital and ended up rushing her to the emergency room. We stayed with her for several hours, holding her hair while she threw up, waiting to be treated, doing our best to love and comfort her in this bad spot. Doctors noticed her as a regular patient and tried to place labels on her immediately. We made sure they treated her with the utmost care and respect she deserved.

We had conversations with the doctors, we told them it would be easy to treat her like a person who is strung out and a label, but we said, "You know she is a person of real worth, who has had a challenging life. She has made a poor choice. Please treat her as if it was your child and not a label." This got their attention immediately, and their attitude towards her and her care shifted. She received the medical treatment needed while staying overnight. She had survived another day. A miracle!

My husband and I asked to meet with her a few days later upon her release. We loved her too much to watch her stay the same. Jessica was hesitant and full of shame because of what had happened. We let her know we loved her, it didn't matter, and we were happy to be there for her. She was broken and more open than ever before to hear what we had to say. We loved her at her darkest and worst hour, but we saw the beauty and destiny she could have. My husband asked her, "What is it going to cost you if you keep living like this?" I asked her if she would give God a chance to change her life, heal her, and bring wholeness.

That day our questions were her turning point; she courageously surrendered to receive help and see what God's love could do for her. Jessica checked in to a recovery center for young women called Mercy Ministries. She opened her life to God's love. For six months, she was in a place that spoke God's love and freedom over her, and it radically changed her.

She needed to be at this recovery center, at this exact time, more than she would ever know. A few months into her life-changing program, her daughter was given just a few days to live. Jessica could be by her side, loving her daughter, and this time as a free woman. Jessica was getting free internally by receiving God's love while facing the most painful devastation of her life - losing her daughter.

In her deepest pain, she didn't run to her pills, and she didn't try to escape her pain. She ran right into God's love. There she found the strength to make her daughter proud of who she was. Jess knew God accepted her; she was in right standing with God because she gave Him the ashes of her life and let God turn them into something beautiful. Jessica felt like her daughter held on to live long enough to see her mama free.

Jessica is a miracle, and to this day, she is one of the most loving people I know. If you met her, you would see that she wears a beautiful smile on her face and a twinkle in her eyes. She lives purposefully and passionately; she works with disabled people and brings honor and life to them.

She writes poems that are powerful and meaningful. I am so thankful she is in my life. God's love has transformed her life to the extent that if I didn't tell you her story, you would have never guessed the life she has lived. It is that impacting!

My friend had amazing breakthroughs when she decided to open her heart to healing. She was taken on a journey to know who God is, and her heart was open to healing when she embraced forgiveness. You, too, can forgive yourself because God forgives you; it makes God happy when you freely accept His gift. If we focus on our weaknesses, we become weak, but we become strong through Him when we focus on His forgiveness and strength. Stop punishing yourself! Nothing good will come from that; good only comes from God. You can accept His goodness over your life.

Think about some things that you hold yourself captive to. It might be a place where you find yourself continually seeing your life through mistakes or past failures. Write down that you will decide today to forgive yourself and live in God's forgiveness. You don't have to run away from regret or hide in your shame; you don't have to allow your past to control your future.

DAILY PRAYER:

Jesus, today, I want to receive your forgiveness and love in a new way. Thank you that you took my sin and punishment upon yourself and instead gave me liberty. I want to walk in the reality that this was an act of your outrageous love, for it was a gift. I want my heart to be free from guilt and accusations towards myself. Break me free from the prison of unforgiveness I've had towards myself. I give up punishing myself. Give me real understanding that you don't see my past failures anymore, but they are under the blood you shed on the cross. Today I let go and won't look back. I am made new. I am in right standing with you. Thank you that your love is transforming my life. Amen.♥

DAILY CHALLENGE:

Like my friend Jessica, you are a product of your past, but the good news is that you don't have to be a prisoner of it! Your past does not limit God's purpose; He can turn it all around for you, just as He did for Jess. You can forgive yourself today by receiving Christ's forgiveness. Make that choice now!

Take the time to forgive yourself. On the next page make a list of what you need to forgive yourself for.

Fill in the blank below:

I forgive myself for

×

×

×

×

×

×

×

I will not hold myself hostage any longer.

God forgives me so I can forgive myself!

Forgive Others

Forgiving others is not popular in our culture. We write songs about getting back at exes and the haters who have wronged us. Revenge by taking justice into our own hands has become about burning people's stuff, slashing their tires, putting out slanderous information on them, or getting even some other way. We have gone down this road for many of us only to find ourselves still hurting, and the problem yet hasn't gone away.

The truth is that if we want to live free and recover wholeness, we must understand the power of forgiveness. It is forgiveness that is the gateway to freedom; it is our human nature to see justice done. We feel that if we forgive, we are letting those who hurt us off the hook, but we are getting them out of our souls. We are letting them off our hook, but they are not off God's hook. Those who hurt you in the past cannot continue to hurt you unless you hold onto the pain through unforgiveness. The past is the past, and nothing can change it.

We must forgive ourselves and others because whatever you allow in your heart has power over you. Unforgiveness can keep you in a prison where you are chained mentally and emotionally to what has been done to you. God wants us to forgive so we can let go of those who have hurt us and not let them have room in our hearts. You don't even have to "feel" like forgiving to forgive. Forgiveness is a choice, not a feeling. When you forgive, you don't have to welcome them back in your life if they are not a healthy person! We can have boundaries and be wise with who we let in our life.

When you forgive, you can start to heal. You will no longer be focused on the negative and injustice that was done to you. Forgiveness is giving God back the right to take care of justice. I have learned that the best way to stay free is when someone has done me wrong; I choose to forgive. I may not FEEL like forgiving, but it is a choice.

I don't want to be chained to anyone. If someone has hurt me and I carry that hurt every day, usually, I am giving them a piece of me. The medical community has recognized that unforgiveness is detrimental to our health. Some cancer centers have started "forgiveness therapy" because science is proving forgiveness has health benefits. According to the Mayo Clinic Online, forgiving improves your health in these ways: improved mental health, less anxiety, decreased stress and hostility, lowered blood pressure, fewer symptoms of depression, a stronger immune system, improved heart health, improved self-esteem, and healthier relationships.

God wants us to forgive, and He already spoke about the power of forgiving people over two-thousand years ago. The truth is that every one of us can find a reason to feel bitter about life, but being bitter is a trap. When You carry a load of toxic thinking, it internalizes all the injustice and negatives in your life. You begin to feel weighed down and unhealthy.

The Bible says bitterness dries up the bones. Your bones help your body move; if your movement is dried up, you become stuck; stuck in life, stuck in pain. People who indulge in bitterness live unhappy lives because they are always carrying a chip on their shoulders. The Bible is full of wisdom that science is now agreeing with. God designed us, and He knew that for us to flourish in life, we must forgive. The good news is you can be free today from those negative feelings. You can choose to let go by daringly say, "I Forgive."

Let this story inspire you to forgive: Scarlett Lewis' son, Jesse, was killed at six years old in the 2012 Sandy Hook Elementary School shooting, the biggest school shooting in U.S. history. At first, she said she felt like her anger sapped all her strength and energy. She was angry at the shooter and the shooter's mother for unwittingly arming him. But she chose to forgive. Scarlett said, "Forgiveness felt like I had been given a big pair of scissors to cut the tie and regain my power. It started with a choice and then became a process." She urged mourners at Jesse's funeral to change their angry thoughts into loving ones that thereby they might change the world. Scarlett went on to create a program in her son's honor called The Choose Love Movement. She turned a tragic situation to help kids like her son's killer learn how to cultivate love. A statement from her website says,

> "An angry thought can be changed. The Choose Love Movement is teaching children and adults how they can choose love. The Sandy Hook tragedy started with an an- gry thought in the shooter's head. But we can change

those angry thoughts into loving thoughts. Our mission is to teach kids that they have control over their thoughts and put them to work for them. Making kids aware that they have the power to control their thoughts and all the benefits of turning their angry thoughts into loving thoughts."

Scarlett's no-cost program has been downloaded more than thirty-thousand times in all fifty states and nearly eighty countries. She forgave a horrific tragedy and turned her pain into power.

Who do you need to forgive, so you are not held by anger? Take some time, to be honest with yourself and ask God to show you if you're carrying unforgiveness and bitterness in your heart. It could be through disappointments, someone who broke your heart, or evil done to you. God will heal your pain if you let Him. Two powerful words, "I forgive," will release you from bitterness and open your heart up to a new level of freedom!

DAILY CHALLENGE:

1.) As an exercise, you can get a sheet of paper and list the names of people that come to your mind that have hurt or offended you. *At this point, don't question whether you should forgive them or not.*

2.) Write down any thoughts you had against God on your list. He has never done anything wrong, so we don't have to forgive Him. Sometimes though, we harbor angry thoughts against Him because He might not have done what we wanted Him to do. Those feelings of anger and resentment can become a wall between Him and us, so we must let them go.

Remember, forgiveness is an act of your own will. It is a decision, not a feeling.

DAILY PRAYER:

Say this prayer for each person you wrote down:

Jesus, I forgive_____.

Thank You for forgiving me for my sins. I freely forgive them and release them to You. I ask You to heal the hurt and pain in me. I don't want them to be bitter cancer in my soul any longer. I want to be free from the prison of unforgiveness. I trust You to bring peace and justice to my life. Thank You that Your love is transforming my life. Amen.♥

You are Enough!

You are enough! You may think you were born in the wrong family, you don't have the looks or the gifts of someone else, but there is something special about you! Not one person, not even twins, share the same fingerprint. There has never been, nor will there ever be another you!

> *"For we are God's handiwork, created in Christ Jesus to do good works, which God prepared in advance for us to do."*
> Ephesians 2:10 [NIV]

Do you think God designs things just to be ok? Have you ever seen the waterfalls in Hawaii or the earth from an airplane? What about the pink cotton candy sunsets on summer nights? These are magnificent masterpieces by God, but His most significant design was you! We are God's handiwork and work of art. We were created to do good things on this planet that God planned long before our arrival. If anyone has ever made you feel not enough or told you that you were not significant, it is time to start believing the One who created you. You are accepted and loved by Him!

Everyone craves to be celebrated and be significant. The world's system tells you to sell out to be celebrated or do whatever is necessary to feel important. Girls will pose naked on social media for more followers and say it's a way of expressing themselves. But what is it that they want? Do they want to be known for their great body, and that is their legacy? Could it be the lack of feeling significant, and that attention is gratifying?

God never intended us to get our self-worth from our bodies or anything superficial. He wants us to take care of our bodies, and there is nothing wrong with looking good, but our bodies should not be our identity. If your label is, "you are the sexiest 20-year-old," and that is where your confidence comes from, what will happen when you start to age, see wrinkles and watch other younger girls take your place? When you turn 30, 40, 50, etc., what is left of your confidence if it's rooted in being a sexy young girl? You begin to realize that your confidence will collapse because you were never meant to find it in surface labels. We are more than our bodies.

God wants our identity to come from Him. He wants to satisfy our need for importance and status throughout His life. In Him, we find our freedom; we find out who we are. When you become secure in God's love, the opinions of other people become irrelevant. Freedom to become all that you have been created to be will be released. Living in this freedom fills the need for acceptance, significance, and satisfaction. You see your need for God to be your source of life because in Him is where you find life. You can climb to the highest level of success and still feel empty because you're missing your source of life. We will never feel satisfied without receiving and owning that God celebrates us.

My friend Jennifer knows all this too well. Many years ago, her life looked like the pinnacle of success. She was on a popular tv show, living in Beverly Hills, California, with her husband and newborn daughter. She was living the Hollywood dream, doing commercials, and being invited to the glamorous red-carpet events. Despite everything she had and was, she felt inside there was more to life. After she went through a painful divorce, hurting and broken, she surrendered to God in a new way.

She knew of God as a young girl, but her soul craved to know God. She realized nothing satisfied her; even though she reached success, most people will only dream. I met her when she was in the midst of her pain and when she decided to pursue God more seriously. I have had the pleasure of watching God transform her life and bring real healing to her soul. She has overcome abuse, an eating disorder, divorce, and depression.

Jennifer has become one of my closest friends, and if you spend time with her, you get to feel real joy and peace in her presence. She is full of life and fully alive! Jennifer is still acting and pursuing her passion. She doesn't measure her success based on the appearance of Hollywood's standards. She has lasting success, and no matter what her life looks like, she is winning on the inside.

I love Jennifer's authenticity. She will share her story to help anyone; she credits her freedom to what God has done. Her pain does not own her anymore, and it has become a power where she encourages others. She is the friend who encouraged me to write this book! Jen had what looked like the ultimate success story in life, but she learned success is measured by knowing God and His standard of freedom. No matter what you think, a successful life looks like, if it doesn't include following Jesus, you will have to spend a lifetime chasing empty fantasies. True freedom is only found in Him.

Your value is not what you do but who you are. Everyone struggles with the need to impress people at some level. Much of the pressure, fear, and stress we experience in our lives is caused by our need to impress others. Can you imagine how free we would be if we didn't worry about what others think about us? How wonderful would it be to know that you don't have anything to prove, and you're satisfied being who God created you to be? Discovering where our actual value comes from helps us take our focus off seeking other's approval. God's approval makes people's approval irrelevant. In the end, we determine where our value comes from.

DAILY PRAYER:

God, I thank you that you chose me, and you made me so you could love me. You gave my life value and worth before anyone could ever diminish it. You designed me just the way I am while I was in my mother's womb. You wanted me, help me to believe this. Help me to prophecy your truth over who you created me to be. Thank you that your love is transforming my life. Amen. ♥

DAILY CHALLENGE:

Write your answers to the questions below and ask God to show you who you are. His voice is always speaking to who you are in His eyes and what you're capable of becoming!

Where are you having the hardest time accepting yourself?

Why are you having a tough time approving of yourself in this area?

Is this causing you to compromise who you are?

How would you feel if you were confident that you were approved and special in God's heart and mind?

Leaving it all Behind

My husband is a speaker and travels for a living. He was invited to speak in Anaheim, California, for a significant business convention with thousands of attendees. I went with him to work since it was not far from our home. He was asked to share a message to inspire people to the wonder of knowing God. It was a moving message. A lady in the audience named Mia thought she was attending a business meeting but had no idea it would change her life. She was moved by what my husband spoke about all God could do for her life. She came to us after the meeting and told us a little about her story. We felt in our hearts to invest in her and meet to talk more. Weeks later, we met together at a cafe, and she began to tell us about her life.

Mia's story began somewhat rocky; as a young girl, she spent a lot of her time in foster care because her mom was an alcoholic. No one was there to protect her; she had to make it on her own. When she was just thirteen years old, she was sexually taken advantage of by a man who was a pimp and seventeen years older than her. That experience left her pregnant and alone.

She had the weight of the world on her shoulders; she was barely a teenager and found out she was pregnant and would be a mom. A scary situation, but she made a bold decision to keep her son even though there were odds she would need to overcome. She shared how the years following were challenging. She didn't want her son to lack anything. At that time, she thought the best thing to do was to become an escort to provide financially for her and her son. She became a prostitute for fifteen years.

At the time that we met her, she was exploring a new business being at this conference. Mia knew in her heart that something deeper had to change than just a career. She knew there was something more for her life, and she wanted it. We shared with her how God desired to give her a good future, and all she had to do was receive God's grace in the person of Jesus.

On the way to meet us, she said voices were telling her God did not care about her and drive her car off the road. She ignored the voices, and that afternoon, at lunch, she said yes to God! She knew that she would need to let go of what held her back if she made this decision. She knew she needed not just to believe Jesus, but follow Jesus. She caught a vision that God could change her life and make it into something beautiful. With a promising future in sight, she walked away from her past and got around people who could push her into her future.

My husband had the opportunity to baptize Mia and was amazed as she forgave herself and those who had hurt her in her past. She indeed became a new person! The tough choices she made were not rewarded with instant results, but she pushed through. If you met her today, you would see that she is one of the kindest, generous, and life-giving people I know.

Mia lives in freedom and gets to experience God's goodness. She has gone on to help other women and inspire them with her story. She has even helped her mom turn her life around from her addiction. Her son is a well-respected man who has followed his mother's example in trusting God and treating others with honor. Not only is she gold on the inside, but Mia has also gone on to be an entrepreneur owning multiple businesses and even does winery tours in Napa, CA. She is recognized and known as the best at what she does!

I love that she had every reason to sit and settle in a life of victimhood and bitterness, but she decided who she could be was more than what she was living. Once she captured a glimpse of her future, she let go of everything that weighed her down so she could pursue a God-designed life.

Are there things God is asking you to give up or people in your life weighing you down? Do you need to take a stand and cut the ties? Our culture's anthem is "YOLO" (you only live once), "do what you feel," "live like it was your last day," "experience it all." I am certainly for enjoying and living life to the fullest, but the anthem for YOLO can be a trap.

God teaches us that what we sow, we will reap. If you make decisions based on how you feel in the moment, to live only for this moment, you can end up paying for them later. God has given us guidelines for our protection. His guidelines protect our heart, hope, and future so that we can build a sturdy and robust life. Whatever you are doing now will affect your tomorrow! There are times in our lives that we don't feel comfortable being the person we use to be; God is stretching us to become more. One of the most significant influences in your life will be your circle; Jesus had a circle of disciples and people with who He spent the most time. Who are you spending the most time with?

"Walk with the wise and become wise, for a companion of fools suffers harm." Proverbs13:20 [NIV]

These days we have hundreds of "friends" on social media, which is fine to have, but who is doing life with you? Do your friends speak to your potential, encouraging you, inspiring you to have healthy goals in life? If you want to thrive, you must look at who your company is and see if they weigh you down or lift you higher. There are seasons in our life where we need to distance ourselves from people who keep bringing us back to our "then" when God wants us to live in our "now." If you're going to grow a healthy self-image, pursue relationships with healthy people. Find people that will push you further in life, people that can see you beyond your weaknesses and speak to who God created you to be. God cares about who you let speak into your life. Casual friends are good, but make sure you have advisers and voices of influence to shape who you want to become.

I have had seasons in my life where I had close friends that never wanted to grow and move on in life. God showed me they held me back, and I needed to create distance from anyone holding me back. I gave more time and energy to those who help me focus on my future and where I need to go. It can be painful to create boundaries on who influences your life, but it is worth it. Some of the people you distance from might one day seek you out when they are ready for healing or growth. Nothing can be harder than staying stuck in life and not growing; God made our lives to flourish, expand, and grow. There were many times that Jesus asked people to move forward and not look back. Your future is ahead, and you can't do it alone; you need people to believe in your future!

Other relationships that hold you back can be romantic ones. If you are dating, it is good to tell yourself the truth and ask yourself, "is my relationship forwarding me or just fondling me?" "Are they just staying around for what they can get?" Have the courage to take inventory of your relationship and see if they are suited for the future you desire. When you trust God and let go, He will always give you someone better. It makes Him happy if you can trust Him for the best in life and purpose to live wise.

The same thing could be with old friends who want to take you back to a life you don't live anymore. They could be great people, and it can hurt to distance yourself, but God can help you. He will bring friends that will expand you! I encourage you to look at the three closest people to you. Do the friendships grow you? Encourage you? Are you speaking more about your future than your past? Do your friends push you to be your best? These are the right questions to think about.

Friendships are so powerful, either for the good or bad, because they shape who you will become and how far you will go! When you make decisions to say yes to God's best, even in relationships, God will reward your faith.

"As iron sharpens iron, so one person sharpens another.
" Proverbs 27:17 [NIV]

DAILY PRAYER:

God, I ask You to fill me with Your wisdom. Holy Spirit, be my guide and help me give up the influences and anything holding me back in life. Teach me Your ways and help me to not live for the temporary but live in the light of eternity. Be my strength in my weakness and fill me with the courage to say "yes" when You want me to say "yes" and "no" when You want me to say "no." Thank You that Your love is transforming my life. Amen.♥

DAILY CHALLENGE:

Today, think about who and what is influencing you the most right now.

Who are your three closest friends?

×

×

×

What are the three most important things to you right now?

×

×

×

Who is speaking to your potential and your future?

×

×

×

If the people or influences are not acceptable, then think about people you should be closer to. Write them down and make sure you connect with them!

×

×

×

Emotions

God never meant for us to live on an emotional roller coaster—riding a "high" when life is good but a "downward spiral" when things don't go as expected. His desire is for us to enjoy His peace and stability through every season of life. We should strive to be emotionally stable. Negative emotions can trigger us to get mad in an instant, fear in a heartbeat, and drive us to self-indulgence. But did you know Jesus taught us that we can oversee our emotions, that the negative emotions do not have to rule us? We should seek God to learn how to manage our emotions and not allow them to manage us.

Imagine this, you go shopping and see a big sale at your favorite store! You promised yourself you were going to pay off your student loan and not spend extra money. You just got too excited about the sale and ended up spending all the money you were saving on new clothes. You gave in to your excitement over a purchase and let your emotions rule instead of leaning on wisdom and ruling your feelings.

Or maybe you had a bad week; everything that could go wrong went wrong, and you decide to sink into a pity party. We all have those weeks! You start rehearsing all the reasons why you have suffered in life, and you let your bad experiences of the week spiral you down into feeling sorry for yourself. You spiral so far down to the point that oppression starts to fill your mind. You start blaming other people and become very moody and unpleasant to be around. You can become so miserable you can look for a temporary fix to numb your pain. This is a trap! Don't let your emotions make your decisions and lead you to a dark place. You can learn to rule your feelings instead of allowing your emotions to run out of control.

"A sound mind makes for a robust body, but runaway emotions corrode the bones." Proverbs 14:30 [MSG]

How do most people handle their emotions or feelings? Our daily lives are defined by the feelings we feel. What we do is usually not based on our ability or skill; it's based on how we feel. Consider comparing frustration, anger, resentment, depression to joy, passion, contentment, excitement, or ecstasy.

We all have feelings, and sometimes they are strong, but we're wrong if we think we must be guided and directed by them.

We don't have to allow our feelings to determine our decisions and, ultimately, our destiny. Often, we believe that if we feel discouraged, we are discouraged; if we feel depressed, we must be depressed. Your feelings are emotions, not reality. In other words, just because you feel a certain way doesn't make that feeling a fact.

I know many people who don't feel loved by God, but that is how they feel, and that feeling is not the truth. If you are not wise with your emotions, the enemy will gain ground in your life when he can convince you that you are your feelings. God wants us to recognize that we are not our feelings and emotions. It's okay to feel them but I'd like to remind you that you are not what you feel right now but what you decide. God wants you to take charge of your emotions rather than simply wish they didn't exist.

"Do you want to be a mighty warrior? It's better to be known as one who is patient and slow to anger. Do you want to conquer a city? **Rule over** *your temper before you attempt to rule a city."* Proverbs 16:32 [TPT]

Whether we experience positive or negative feelings is usually determined by the thoughts and meanings we connect and agree with concerning events or relationships. If you attach a purpose that where you are is the beginning of something great, you will feel a certain set of emotions that could be empowering. Yet, if you choose to attach a mindset of "nothing ever works out for me," you will get another set of emotions; these emotions will drain and defeat you.

We feel not based on the circumstance we are in, but on how we interpret and define the experience. Some of us try our best to avoid our emotions, and others try to endure them; I believe there is a better way. Through the power of God's Spirit, we can rule over the emotions that weaken us, and we can embrace the ones that empower our lives.

How do you want to feel right now? I have found that when you get clear about how you want to feel, you begin to move in that direction. Here is a question I found helpful when dealing with my feelings: What would you have to believe or focus on to feel the way you have been feeling? If you feel discouraged or defeated, your focus has been on what did not work out or how someone did not treat you right. On the contrary, if you feel empowered, you have shifted your focus on what God is doing in your life and not on what hasn't happened. Know that when you shift, your attention can quickly change the way you feel.

For a minute, I want you to recall a specific time when you felt negative feelings or emotions, and you overcame them. Do you have it in your mind? By remembering a time when you were able to deal with the negative emotions, it will reassure you that you can deal with them now.

The two most negative feelings we all encounter consistently are fear and anger. I have discovered that while these feelings can present themselves to us throughout the day, we have the fruit of self-control that allows us to overcome and live beyond them. I have found that when I become grateful on purpose and focus on all the blessings in my life and how far God has brought me, the two destructive emotions can't operate. I have also discovered that when I replace expectations with appreciation in my life, I have experienced the most peace, joy, and fulfillment. God's Word encourages us not to be overcome by evil but to overcome evil with good.

I am married to a happy man; I have known him to always be a positive person. He wakes up in a good mood and sees life through happy lenses. He often wakes up and says out loud, "This is the day the Lord has made; I will rejoice and be glad in it!" He is making a declaration that he will rejoice and be glad, and he does! He is not consulting his feelings to decide what kind of day he is going to have. He is in control. I love this about him.

> " A joyful, cheerful heart brings healing to both body and soul. But the one whose heart is crushed struggles with sickness and depression. " Proverbs 17:22 [TPT]

A cheerful mind is powerful and will bring healing to you. A broken spirit that is filled with worry, fear, anxiety, shame, guilt, regret, and dread will crush your life and stop momentum where you become stuck. If you daily live in any one of these emotions, they are toxic to who you were created to be. God does not want you to live in brokenness. He has a remedy for every broken piece to your life; when you give Him your ashes, He will return them for beauty.

Sometimes a broken spirit is consumed in grief, due to loss in life. We all go through the pain of loss and grief is a normal emotion to feel. It's healthy to grieve over the loss of a loved one or even a life you once had. But grief cannot become a lifestyle, it's meant to be for a season. The bible says there is a time, a season appointed for everything. Seasons do change, God did not intend winter to last forever so He made Spring. That is why He made a remedy for grief.

"... and provide for those who grieve in Zion—to bestow on them a crown of beauty instead of ashes, the oil of joy instead of mourning, and a garment of praise instead of a spirit of despair..." Isaiah 61:2-3 [NIV]

If you are struggling with a lifestyle of mourning or grief and you know the season has lasted too long, God has an antidote. And He is willing and able to meet you in your pain. Beauty, joy and praise are waiting for you. Pray with someone who can speak life over you. Ask God for strength and study His Word to discover His love that will transform emotions that are hurting you. God's strength and wisdom will help you live by your decisions, not your feelings.

"He heals the brokenhearted. And binds up their wounds [healing their pain and comforting their sorrow]."

Psalm 147:3 [AMP]

DAILY PRAYER:

God, thank you that you want me to be healthy in my emotions. I don't want to live in despair or be controlled by anger, jealousy, sulking, or fear. Heal me from emotions that are hurting me. Teach me to have a cheerful, sound, and stable mind. Heal my toxic emotions and give me your grace to be led by your Spirit and not my feelings. Set me free from negative thought patterns and strongholds in my mind. I receive the healing available to my soul. Thank you that Your love is transforming my life. Amen.♥

DAILY CHALLENGE:

Today I want you to remember a time that you felt a negative emotion, and you were able to shift that feeling, not based on your circumstances, but your choices. Maybe it was dealing with fear, and you changed your thoughts to faith. I want you to see that you can rule your emotions. If you have a reoccurring toxic emotion that you struggle with on a weekly or daily basis, write it down and ask yourself how you can shift.

Your Relationship with God

Of all the relationships in your life, the most important one is your relationship with God. Love and relationships start and begin with Him, for love is who He is, not just something He gives. Before you were born, he designed you out of love. That's right—even if you were born through an adverse circumstance or to a parent who didn't want you or intended to have you, God planned you. You are not some mass-produced or manufactured idea, but deliberately selected and precisely put together. Every person is a brand-new idea from the mind of God.

Think about it for a minute: You exist simply because He wills you to exist. Since you were made by Him and for Him, living disconnected from Him will leave you feeling dissatisfied. Isn't a relationship with God what you truly desire—a relationship with someone who can see all that's good and bad about you and still love you unconditionally?

Let me offer further insight to help and empower you: it's a part of God's character to think well of you. God sees your whole reality and says, "I love you, I want you, and I'm only interested in doing you good." He knows you don't do everything right; that's why He sent Jesus to reconcile you to Himself so you could receive His love and He could love you affectionately.

Accepting God's love is pursuing a friendship with Him. The Bible says, "Draw near to God, and He will draw near to you." He wants to have constant conversations with us. He doesn't want to just be a part of a morning routine, but He wants to be a part of every activity, thought, and action. He wants to have an open conversation with us throughout the day. You might just be getting to know God, or you have known of Him your whole life. In my own life, I have discovered how important it is to God that He doesn't just want me to know about Him. He wants me to *know* Him. The God of this whole universe is interested in knowing you and being your friend!

Jesus said in John 15:15, *"No longer do I call you servants, for the servant does not know what his master is doing; but I have called you friends, for all that I have heard from my Father I have made known to you."*

Some people think a relationship with God is a master and servant experience, but God wants us to know who He is, what He likes, and what He is doing! How do you know what God is doing? You know what God is doing by studying His Word, talking to Him throughout the day (prayer,) and in worship.

Worship and prayer connect our hearts to God. When we. live this lifestyle, we get to experience His presence, His love, His peace, and Him being near us; it is a way we connect closely with God. When we read the Bible, we discover who God is, and His Word brings life to us; His Word directs us to live in truth. The truth always produces well in our life even though sometimes it can be hard to face the truth; it is the ultimate way to live. Where there is truth, it will produce freedom.

"Your word is a lamp to my feet and a light to my path."
Psalm 119:105 [NIV]

God's Word lights our world, and it gives us direction; it helps us move forward in life and put one foot in front of the other! God did not design us to look back in our past; He is always pushing us forward.

The more you pursue God, you discover His character; you see how God is patient and loving, how He works with us even in our weakness and limitations. Remember, God is not surprised by our flaws; He knows you and is committed to you. When we read and get in His Word, He gives us a picture of who we can be, and it's like looking in a mirror at our potential. He is the friend that can see us at our worst but still believes the best of us. The best way to read the Bible is by reading it while knowing God is loving, and He's always good.

God cannot be compared to any human relationship because He promises never to leave us or forsake us. Even when others leave us, He promises never to walk out on us. God is good to us even when we don't deserve it; He loved us before we chose to love Him. Knowing His love and walking with Him is the only way to experience a satisfying life. Our soul craves to experience Him, and it's what transforms us.

I love to write my prayers and what God is speaking to me in a journal. It is incredible to look back in my journals and see my prayers answered, to see how God was speaking to me. One of the big prayers I had written was what I desired in a husband. I knew I did not want to settle in life because I wanted to have a special marriage that lasted a lifetime. Many years before meeting my husband, I set my heart to be married to someone passionate about me and passionate about helping people. I had a long, specific list with important qualities in a man along with some silly desires.

Many years before meeting my husband, one of the playful things I wrote was to marry someone who lives in California and who lives on the beach. While I was living in Canada, I did not know anyone who lived in California. You might say that's an unimportant desire, or God does not care about details like that. But God made it happen!

When I met my husband Rex, it was a story for the fairytale books. I knew God gave me the ultimate because I didn't settle for just anyone and didn't care how long it took. I wanted God's best. God gave me the best; He gave me all the essential traits I wanted in a man. He even gave me someone who lived in California on the beach! When you become close to God, you will learn that He enjoys giving you your heart's desires.

"Delight yourself in the Lord, and He will give you the desires of your heart." Psalms 37:4 [NIV]

One of the greatest blessings Rex and I desired was to have a child. When I got pregnant, I knew my baby was a gift from God. Since I have a mechanical heart valve, it was not easy carrying a child. I had to replace my oral blood thinner medicine, which could cause birth defects, with an injection. I had to give myself an injection directly into the fleshy part of my stomach or thigh twice a day for nine months.

I became covered in painful black and blue bruises. I was considered a "high risk" pregnancy, so I had to visit the prenatal every week, which was fine, except the doctors were concerned for my health and repeatedly asked if I wanted to terminate my pregnancy. This was not an enjoyable experience to be regularly reminded of their fears. Especially since I had no complications other than my bruises and the typical pregnancy ailments like morning sickness and backaches.

My husband and I believed in a miracle, and I told the doctors I would not be terminating my miracle. Sometimes miracles can be hard to push out into the world, but with God, His strength sustains us. I needed this strength when I was in labor. After too many hours of labor, I had to be taken in for an emergency C-section. For some reason, even with the usual drugs, when they were cutting me open, I could feel it, and I was screaming, but they thought I was just dramatic. My husband knew something was wrong because it's not my personality to be dramatic.

The nurse gave me more laughing gas, but it didn't work, and I started to lift out of my body into light. I could see myself on the operating room table as my body was in the light. It felt so good to be in this presence, and I didn't want to go back. For some reason, I knew this was what it would be like stepping into heaven and God's presence. But without a choice, I returned to my body, and within seconds my focus went from pain to extreme joy when I got to meet my precious baby, which we named Kira! My husband and I were in tears. God fulfilled a desire, and we were holding her in our arms. It wasn't easy to bring her to the world, but she was worth the fight.

My relationship with God helped sustain me through every step. He was the constant strength. He gave me the boldness to tell the doctors, "I'm going to keep my miracle," He gave me the strength to endure the injections. He even rescued me in my pain and gave me an out of body experience in His light!!

Staying close to God always leads to a life of miracles. You're about to give birth to new things. Miracles are in motion for you, though you might feel resistance and obstacles keep following the motion of your miracle. Your faith is stronger than your feelings. You're about to give birth to brand new things!

Pursuing a real relationship with God has been the most rewarding relationship I have ever sought. It has not been about following rules but caring about what He cares about, and He cares about being close to us. For any relationship to work, you must be committed and invested. I know many people who settle for a causal relationship with God, yet this always ends in frustration. As for God, He is committed to you! He gets more glory out of your life being a success rather than a failure, yet, for this relationship to manifest its potential, He asks for a commitment from us.

The Scripture says two cannot walk together unless they agree or make an appointment. This is your date with destiny! Will this be the moment that you decide once and for all that you are more than what you are living? Will this be the day you take the hand of Jesus, who is the way so that He can lead you into the abundant and overflowing life He always dreamed of you having? You were born to be alive at this time. God has adventures and miracles waiting for you. Keep your "yes" big to Him and watch your life transform from the inside out!

DAILY PRAYER:

God, I desire to not just know about you but to know you closely. Fill me with your spirit today, so I can feel you and see you in a new way. I ask that you show me any area of my heart which I need to surrender to you. Help me to read your word and let it come alive in my life. Help me to pray and talk to you throughout the day. I want an open dialogue, a real friendship. Help me to hear your voice and feel your love every day of my life. Guide me into truth and let my life reflect yours. I want people to know I've encountered the God of the Universe and see your love and miracles in my life. Thank you that your love is transforming my life. Amen. ♥

DAILY CHALLENGE:

What are the ways that you may be living less than God has called you to live?

What are some ways that you can pursue a deeper relationship with God?

What are the ways that you can see how God has pursued you?

List some things that you have always dreamed of for your life but have not yet seen come to pass? Pray over these things and speak life into them. Agree that God will always have your best interest at heart!

ABOUT THE AUTHOR

Katrina is passionate about life and loves to inspire women through her story. Overcoming a fatal disease and fighting through; abuse, an eating disorder, and depression, Katrina is a bright voice of life on the other side of pain. Her story has been shared with girls in the red-light district in Thailand to businesses in the United States, schools, churches, and her former published, print magazine. Her greatest titles are being a wife and a mom. She is married to her best friend, Rex. Katrina and Rex are proud parents to their miracle daughter, Kira Jewel. They live in sunny Southern California.

You can follow her on social media: @katrinacrain

Made in the USA
Middletown, DE
29 August 2024

59857206R00075